# Complete

# Aries 2021

## Monthly astrological forecasts for 2021

**TATIANA BORSCH**

Translated from Russian by Sonja Swenson-Khalchenia
Translation copyright © Coinflow Limited, Cyprus
AstraArt Books is an imprint of Coinflow limited, Cyprus
Published by Coinflow Limited, Cyprus
For queries please contact: tatianaborsch@yahoo.com
ISBN 978-9925-579-30-3 (paperback)
ISBN 978-9925-579-31-0 (ebook)

# Contents

# 2021 - Birth of a New World

Based on the events of this year, my 2020 predictions, which were published on my website and in *SWAAY* magazine, are coming true (I write this article in summer 2020). We are bearing witness to an era of change; the world is teetering on the brink, and everything we thought was permanent and unshakable has turned out not to be. What else lies ahead?

It is impossible to separate the events of 2020 and 2021. These are years of major shifts, with an effect on each country, each home, and each individual. 2020's developments will continue in 2021, and there is simply no equivalent in modern history. It's safe to say that mankind has not experienced these kinds of changes in a very long time.

Major astrological events during this period are:

*The first conjunction of Saturn and Jupiter in the air element will take place in Aquarius.* This extremely significant event will literally take place as 2020 becomes 2021- on December 25, 2020.

This means the dawn of the Age of Aquarius, which almost everyone has heard about.

The Age of Aquarius is very long, lasting 2,160 years. It is determined by the Earth's shift from one axis to another. This transition period from one age to another can last a long time. Many astrologists believe that it will last at least 100 years. The last 20 years have been turbulent- they were vital preparation for the adoption of new rules for a new era.

All of this means that 2020 is the last year of the outgoing Age of Pisces, and 2021 is the first year of the Age of Aquarius.

Shifting eras is always linked with global shocks, crises of civilization, and economic and cultural revolutions, as well as a new perspective on religious teachings. Even the climate usually undergoes major changes.

Summer and autumn 2020, and all of 2021, are clear indicators of that.

The second most important astrological phenomenon is conflict between Saturn and Uranus, which will continue throughout 2021.

Saturn will square Uranus several times in 2021 – we can divide them into the following periods: January-March, May-the first half of July, December 2021-January 2022.

During these periods, we can expect many problems to rear their heads. It is hard to say exactly how this will influence each individual person as part of a general prediction – everything depends on your personal data, though, generally speaking, I can say that we will see the following trends in during these periods of 2021:

I.    First of all, we can expect the economic crisis to expand in scope. Many people will lose their jobs, and companies will go bankrupt.

II.   In many countries, we will see social breakdown. People will organize strikes and demonstrations, and the overarching theme will be their discontent with authorities and the current order. We will see confrontation between society and power structures.

III.  In global hotspots, we may see new deployments of military force or reescalation of conflict.

IV.   For individuals, problems that began in 2019 or 2020 will continue, though this time, things may worsen. Remember – a chain is only as strong as its weakest link.

V.    The climate may undergo significant changes- flooding and forest fires will cause extensive damage. Large-scale migrations will be the result. In response, governments of countries in a better position may declare states of emergency or deploy troops in order to prevent unwanted migrants from crossing their borders.

VI. This interaction between Saturn and Uranus is indicative of conflict between old and new ways of life, and a difficult, irreconcilable struggle that will be reflected in all areas of life – social, economic, and political.

Saturn carries the energy of restrictions and structure. At the same time, Uranus is the planet of unexpected, revolutionary change (as well as high tech). Conflict between the two planets leads to sharp changes in existing reality. Transitioning to a new world and a new set of rules will lead to conflict.

Interaction between Saturn and Uranus speaks to opposition to both new and old ways of living, and of the rigid, irreconcilable struggle that is reflected in every sphere of life – social, economic, and political. Most peoples' lives will undergo dramatic changes, and they will have to adapt.

# Economics and Politics

Saturn will square Uranus throughout 2021, and this will raise difficult questions – it is time for out with the old, in with the new. But replacing an old system with a new one is rarely a peaceful process. That is why the struggle between old and new economic orders will be a feature of 2020 and 2021.

Former economic systems will begin to transform, right before our very eyes, and these processes will go hand in hand with trade wars, political reckoning, and in some cases, armed conflict.

As the global financial crisis further unfolds, we can expect to see a stronger China, and weakened United States. Countries in the Western financial system will suffer greatly, particularly those in the Eurozone, and American political and economic satellites.

From an astrological perspective, the American presidential elections will take place during one of the most challenging periods of 2020. By now, we are used to political scandals every four years when they occur. However, I fear that the 2020 elections will put all others to shame when it comes to political upheaval.

On Election Day and the period leading up to it, Mercury and Mars will be in retrograde, which means that there will be significant incorrect or intentionally twisted information, crowds of protesters, and this will peak the last week before the elections take place, on November 3. Retrograde planets also point toward the opposition party trying to protest the election results, which will translate into large-scale scandal.

Donald Trump may be re-elected for a second term, if Joe Biden is his only opponent. Incriminating information on Biden will come to light in late September or October 2020, when he will simultaneously battle serious health issues. Generally speaking, Biden's horoscope is much weaker than Trump's.

Whoever ends up as President of the United States will have to face a series of problems in 2021- most of all conflict among members of his inner circle.

The horoscope of the United States, which was founded on the day of its Declaration of Independence, on July 04, 1776, in Philadelphia, Pennsylvania, USA, predicts that America's economic and political might will waste away, and this may take place more quickly than we can imagine.

This crisis in the American system will lead to a drop and depreciation in the US dollar in late 2020 or the first quarter of 2021. The US chart suggests that in 2021, the dollar will be replaced as a reserve currency.

As America weakens, it will face growing confrontations with other countries. In 2021, the US will wield less influence on political and economic allies.

There may even be tides of separatism within the States themselves.

Even so, I do not think the United States is threatened by the same fate as the USSR – it is unlikely to disintegrate. But it is possible that in late 2020 or early 2021, some states will declare their desire to secede, and even take some decisive steps in that direction, but full secession is not in the cards. Nonetheless, the struggle will be very difficult for America's political elite and society as a whole.

Large-scale social protests and unrest, which we saw in 2019 and 2020 will continue in 2021, though they may become more aggressive in nature.

This does not only apply to the United States. Social activism will grow worldwide. Mottos of the Age of Aquarius are FREEDOM, EQUALITY, and BROTHERHOOD, and they will be brandished in many countries around the world. This time, the conflict will not only be over ethnic or racial issues, but also pit social classes against each other – the rich versus the poor.

During the second half of 2020, and nearly all of 2021, expect an economic crisis that will spare nearly no country around the world. Many will blame their current governments, and brutal confrontations between citizens and the authorities will follow, oppositions will become active, demonstrations will take place, and instability in some countries may go so far as to topple current regimes.

England will also be dragged into financial crisis, and according to its horoscope, the worst period countrywide is likely to begin in December 2020, and last until September 2023. Expect financial problems, changes in the Royal Family (the Queen is likely to leave the throne between December 2020 and July 2021), and also innovative changes to how the country is governed.

There are also indications that in the summer and fall of 2020, a financial crisis is likely in the Russian Federation, and it will continue into 2021.

During this period, President Putin's horoscope contains indications of a systemic crisis, financial shortages, and growing opposition movements. Any leader's horoscope is largely a reflection of the state of his or her country.

# Money

All countries will lean more strongly toward virtual currencies and cryptocurrencies, which will be accepted by many countries' governments over the next three to five years. This will make it easier to control cash flow, and with it, all of us.

Our reality will increasingly take place virtually, and professionals in this arena will make up the most sought-after and highly-paid class of workers.

As far as personal finance, the Zodiac sign horoscopes included in my book, "Complete Horoscope 2021" offer more specific information. But generally speaking, during a transition period, it is better to refrain from taking risks, and best to avoid investing your money in get-rich-quick schemes.

What's more, there is a saying "Don't risk your house on a sure thing"-now, that is surprisingly relevant.

# Personal life

A crisis is a crisis, but love is an eternal concept. So long as humans exist, they will live and love. 2021 will likely also be a year of major changes in this arena. While tragedy will befall some, others will find happiness.

Unstable partnerships are likely to fall apart, and all the problems faced by unhappy couples are likely to rear their ugly heads.

Unexpected breakups are a possibility, and in many cases, this will be related to an existential crisis, internal discomfort, or maybe even material losses.

Couples with a sincere bond and real affection for one another may be able to take their relationship to the next level, for example, they may begin living together, or get married.

The political, economic, and social shifts underway might force many to move, find a new place to live, or acquire real estate. Many people may also find themselves immersed in issues related to housing- buying or restoring a home, and in some cases, that may be related to moving to another city or even abroad.

In that scenario, be careful and pay attention- due to the conflict between Saturn and Uranus, it is not worth making any investments in a completed construction or second home unless the project has already been proven.

People will begin to seriously reconsider their views on the concept of marriage in the near future. During the Age of Aquarius, bonds between people will be built on ideas of equality and spiritual unity.

The current trend of increasing numbers of non-traditional relationships will only grow stronger.

Differences between the sexes will gradually fade away, as Aquarius is the sign of unisex. Marriage itself will begin to resemble the classic model less and less, as it becomes free, and in some cases, "open". This may bring both advantages and serious disadvantages. Obviously, freedom is a good thing. But that freedom often goes hand in hand with loneliness.

Conflict between Saturn and Uranus will lead to a generational conflict. Saturn represents the older generation, parents, while Uranus represents rebellious children. That means that the younger generation will actively push back against pressure from their elders, and the older generation will need to become wiser and more flexible.

# Health

Technology will play a greater role in medicine, affecting every branch of it.

The union of Saturn and Jupiter, and their tension toward Uranus suggest unexpected deaths, which may be due to various types of accidents and cataclysms.

Those suffering from chronic cardiovascular or spinal diseases should take special precautions.

We may encounter a "second wave" of coronavirus, or outbreaks of new, unknown diseases.

I entitled this article "Birth of a New World". Birth is a painful process, and a mother's body undergoes significant changes, but the fact remains that birth is a great joy for parents and loved ones. The same can be said for 2021. It will not be an easy year, and many will have a difficult time – whether they face problems at work or in their personal life, but that is the logical continuation of the period we live in. We will gain experience and knowledge, and see the emergence of new technology, which will open a new chapter in human history. I am certain that after a transition period, the Age of Aquarius will be the beginning of a new, wonderful world.

Tatiana Borsch

*July 12, 2020*

# 2021 Overview for Aries

*Things are steadily charging ahead in 2021, and that's for the best, especially for you. The way to the top becomes more difficult, but as they say, "no pain, no gain"!*

**Work.** Without a doubt, the last three years have been kind to you. You've grown at work and are making more money. But 2021 will throw you a curveball, and you'll have to adapt and learn to go with the flow.

No, you're not going to change who you are, and your growing business is going to continue, one way or another. But over the course of the year, you will find yourself grappling with challenging, thorny issues with those from your inner circle, close friends, or your superiors.

This will most likely be with regard to money or other valuable property, and initially, the problem may seem hopeless. You're going to have to come back to it more than once throughout the year. Alternatively, people who have helped you or given favors in the past will be unable to do so in 2021, and you will find yourself handling a lot of problems on your own.

You'll only start to see clear progress in December, but in 2022, things will be looking much brighter- all the difficult, contentious issues will have been resolved one way or another.

The eclipses of 2021 will fall on the part of your sky responsible for relationships in general, and specifically, relationships with faraway places. That means that contacts with colleagues in other cities or abroad will become important. You will see the birth of a full partnership which has the power to totally change both your business and your life.

In some cases, a developing business or new job will make you consider moving to distant places.

New people, new friends, and new partners will appear on your horizon in 2021. This will keep things interesting, and life will keep moving forward, merrily and quickly.

**Money.** When it comes to finances, 2021 might bring both failure and success. The stars recommend paying closer attention to your surroundings, old friends, loved ones, and people with whom you share a common material interest. One of them may cause you to lose a lot of money from time to time.

At the same time, new sources of income may appear, so despite the problems, you will be able to maintain financial balance.

**Love and family.** This year, your personal life is not going to be easy. Many families will see problems involving children. This highly sensitive area of your life will require special attention. It is possible that throughout the year, a large part of your family's budget will end up going toward your children's needs.

Relationships with your relatives will become very important. In all challenging situations this year, you will be able to find support from your closest family members.

2021 will be a difficult year for those in romantic partnership. Their relationships will constantly be put to the test, and the main topic of potential issues, unfortunately, will be money or other material concerns. It's a bad thing when love and money are tied up together, and even worse when that causes problems. Remember that love plays by strict rules, and the more you demand, the less you get. If you follow that, you'll be able to mitigate any situation and come out unscathed.

**Health.** 2021 finds you bounding with energy, and that will help you deal with issues at work and in your personal life.

# January

*"Business before pleasure!" This will be your motto throughout January. And the stars will help you!*

**Work**. January is a time of buzzing activity and overcoming various obstacles. It is a tense, but overall positive time, when you will be able to tackle problems from the past, while also outlining your plans for the future.

Many Aries will have an excellent chance to prove themselves as leaders, able to inspire others and organize them well.

Employees will fall into their bosses' favor, and entrepreneurs will see that promising projects are being promoted.

Still, you wouldn't describe January as "calm". "A fly in the ointment in a barrel of honey" may describe a relationship with an old friend, like-minded people, or influential mentors. It will be over finances, as suddenly, due to the strange position of people you were previously able to trust, and this time, you have a lot to lose. The situation will escalate near the middle of the month, and will continue in the future. Moving forward, the next "D-Day" looks like it will be in late February.

Relationships with associates in other cities or countries will develop with varying success - some things will turn out, and with others you will still have work left to do. But this is a story you've seen before, and you've always managed. You'll do it again.

**Money**. Financially, January is a bit of a conundrum. On one hand, you won't find yourself without money, but on the other, large, unplanned expenses or unexpected losses are likely. In any case, stay away from financial risks, sign any necessary papers in advance, don't make any promises related to money or other material values – following through will not come easily.

**Love and family.** You are immersed in your work this month, and your personal life may end up on the back burner. And this is the best-case scenario. In the worst case, many Aries will experience turbulence and find themselves constantly arguing with those closest to them. This may be over different worldviews and unresolved financial issues.

If this sounds like you, the stars suggest fastening your seatbelts and exercising patience. If you let it all go, these problems may only snowball and lead to serious arguments next month.

It's also possible that a loved one will experience problems, and you will have to help them – with words, deeds, and money.

**Health**. All month, you are healthy, energetic, and enthusiastic. But don't overdo it physically. You run a risk of exhausting yourself and suddenly being injured. The 12th through 28th of January is the most inauspicious time for this.

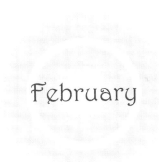

# February

*It seems you took a dead-end road. But don't get too discouraged! There are other paths, and when you need it the most, they will become crystal clear to you.*

**Work**. Your main concern this month will be your relationship with a friend or high-level benefactor. This will involve money or other financial obligations, and, as often happens, each party may have a different version of the events. So long as the situation is not resolved, much of your time will be spent in conflict and quarrels, and thus far, there are no winners.

This may lead to some ambiguity, and your task will be patiently getting through the most difficult periods, which will be frequent this month. You will engage in all sorts of intrigue and nuances here, so pick a strategy and don't lose your cool if things don't turn out the way you'd like.

**Money**. This month may turn out to be devastating. You will be dealing with large expenses all of February, so keep an eye on funds and reduce your risk of losses. Those who work in finance – bankers, accountants, and brokers – should be especially careful. There are no risks worth taking this month, and they will bring nothing but losses.

**Love and family**. Everything is quiet in your personal life, but only as quiet as your life is today. Nonetheless, those in relationships may find themselves growing apart, and married couples will feel friction with their children.

Couples on the rocks (both married couples and those who have not yet walked down the aisle) may start to doubt their future together, but nothing is going to happen yet this month. What's more, confrontation between Mars and Venus will force you to reconsider certain periods in your relationships, as your partner's virtues and shortcomings will come to light.

Love always hopes for the best, though, and it's not worth losing faith over a few bumps in the road.

**Health**. For most of February, you will be feeling rather good, and it is only as of the 27th that you will start to feel sluggish. All month long, your emotions will be up and down, so try to get enough sleep and eat properly.

# March

*The scenery is changing in March, the skies are clearing, and you are feeling calmer. There's a way out of any situation!*

**Work**. March is an ideal time for resolving any difficult situations that recently began. Complaints from your friends or superiors are becoming less relevant- maybe you found a shortcut to reconciliation, or perhaps the problems in question have simply faded away. In any case, things are moving forward for you, and that's already something positive!

During the first twenty days of March, you will be able to calmly resolve any difficult financial issues and receive a handsome sum of money.

The last ten days of the month are a good time to renew contact with colleagues or old friends in other cities or abroad. You might take a trip or start preparing for one.

Employees might take a brief vacation, and restore their nerves and emotions after the obstacles you overcame last month.

**Money**. Your finances are looking up in March. Money will be coming in regularly, and not only from official sources. You can expect support from parents, your spouse, or a loved one. Alternatively, you can count on sponsorship and credit.

**Love and family**. When it comes to your personal life, you can count on one of two differing outcomes. Either you will be able to shelter from the storm under the broad, strong wing of a loved one, or you will find yourself licking your own, self-inflicted wounds.

In any case, March will be a bit calmer than earlier months were. Many Aries who quarreled with their friends and partners earlier will find a way to reconcile. The second half of the month is particularly promising for this. During this period, you might also take a trip, or meet old friends living in other cities or abroad.

**Health**. You might feel less than sure of yourself and cheerful this month. Fortunately, you will have an excellent chance to leave work behind and get some more time to yourself. Take advantage of it, as there will not be many opportunities like it this year.

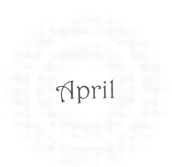

# April

*You're on a winning streak, but that doesn't mean you can sit back and put your feet up. Take initiative, keep looking ahead, and the stars will help you at every turn!*

**Work.** Your main task and true success this month will be developing your relationship with colleagues from other cities or abroad. You are facing almost no barriers, and are supported, necessary, and in demand. There is a real possibility of taking a trip which will be very successful, and will be instrumental in driving your business forward.

You may meet new friends, like-minded and influential benefactors. What's more, you are likely to reestablish old relationships, too. Thanks to your many backers, you are able to carry out your longstanding plans, and (in some cases) even think about moving or acquiring real estate somewhere faraway.

**Money.** Your financial position is looking up, and that will become very apparent the second half of April. During this period, you might see some unexpected successes and real blessings. You might even try your luck and buy a lottery ticket – it will pay off in dividends for the very luckiest.

**Love and family.** Your personal and romantic relationships are also expected to improve significantly. There's no harm in dreaming this month – on the contrary, it's quite useful to you. Single people and those who have been disappointed by past relationships will be particularly lucky. You are highly likely to meet interesting people in every respect in April, and one of them may become your one and only. In many cases, that will happen on a trip, or while with people who have come from afar.

April is also a good month for couples and lovers. Many will have a chance to see a place they had dreamed about for a long time, and that will have a most favorable impact on the relationship.

April is also a good month for reconnecting with old friends and partners, so keep this in mind if you recently broke off ties with someone for various reasons.

**Health**. You are going at full throttle, but despite your busy schedule, you're not feeling tired. You are full of strength, energy, and attention from others will boost your mood and self-esteem.

# May

*Your path is one of constant forward motion, and now, fate has given you no choice. As they say, no pain no gain!*

**Work.** You have always been full of ideas, ambition, and now, you have more than ever! Business is moving ahead, your projects are underway, and you aren't facing any money problems. But luck is rarely ever entirely complete, so right now, a relationship with a friend or superior may be fly in the ointment. Most likely, the issue is money or other, similar financial obligations, and you will have to give up a lot – both this month and a little down the road.

Alternatively, you might just be the victim of fraud, at the hands of people close to you or someone you trust! For that reason, "trust but verify" is more than relevant this month!

Your relationship with colleagues from other cities or countries will become very important; long-term cooperation is likely being planned. In any case, a series of summer eclipses are pointing toward this, and one of them is happening right this month. That cooperation may have only varying success, but with time, you will overcome everything.

**Money.** Finances are going well enough in May; you will have money coming in regularly, and it might be a lot more than usual, too. You will not be able to escape some expenses, most of which are related to the uncompromising stance of a friend or mentor. You may have to give in at some point, as part of fulfilling past obligations, and this part will be excessive.

**Love and family.** Your personal life is stressing you out and jerking you around. Many families were planning building projects, and in some cases, that will take place in another city or abroad. More decisive Aries will be taking their first steps toward making that happen this month, while those who are more measured will plan everything out first, before diving in.

Your relationship with family will become more significant, and you may visit relatives living in other cities or abroad. Many will also meet up with old friends living far away. You may even go on a successful trip.

Single people might expect to be on the receiving end of some attention and romance, which might take place while traveling or among people who have come from somewhere far away.

**Health.** This month, you are feeling energetic and have no reason to fear falling ill.

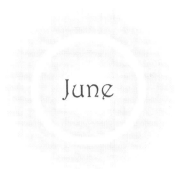

# June

*Pay attention to your surroundings while traveling, and keep your foot off the gas. The later you arrive at your destination, the better. It might be surprising, but right now, that's just how it is!*

**Work.** The eclipse on June 10 will force most Aries, once again, to take a very close look at your associates from other cities or abroad. Even so, you are already used to the bumps in the road ahead. The problem isn't you, but rather the strange and occasionally contradictory behavior of your colleagues. This inconsistency, and potentially even dishonesty, will cause real delays as well as significant losses.

In order to mitigate these issues, it would be a good idea to be prepared early on, as you are fully aware of what is going on.

During this time, you can expect problems involving real estate, or other facilities, especially if you are a manager or entrepreneur.

In addition to this, many Aries will be dealing with intrigue, and unreliable or deliberately misrepresented information in June, so avoid any major decision-making until you get all the details and a clear picture of the situation.

Trips planned for June might not turn out quite as you had planned.

**Money.** Financially, June is not expected to be a particularly pleasant month. In the middle of the month, you might experience heavy losses, due to adverse circumstances, both at work and at home.

**Love and family.** Your personal life is turbulent and full of ups and downs. Your relationship with relatives is extremely tense, you might see unnecessary drama, conversations that go nowhere, and difficult revelations about your relationships. On top of that, your relationship with your children – both yours and your spouse's – is likely to sour. During the middle of the month, you may end up spending large amounts on the younger generation's needs.

Couples will unexpectedly realize that various outlooks on life divide them, along with differing value systems, and, potentially, financial problems. In a word, June is not likely to bring you much peace, anywhere.

**Health.** You are feeling energetic this month and are not expected to fall ill. The stars still strongly urge you to be careful when traveling and driving, as there is a high likelihood of traffic accidents.

# July

*July has you strongly focused on your home life. Things will work out beautifully for you, as long as you are careful and measured in your actions.*

**Work.** This month is more about relaxation and plans with your family, and not particularly promising for work or your career. The exception is those working in construction or whose business is somehow related to real estate, hotels, and recreation.

Entrepreneurs will make a decision about expanding their business, and examine various possibilities for purchasing or renting real estate.

Employees will be more focused on their family this month, and the stars recommend that those who are destined to remain at work refrain from making any requests from the powers that be – now is not the time.

Your relationship with colleagues from other cities or abroad is moving along and changing for the better; some things will turn out, and others will not quite be as you hoped – just like anything else.

**Money.** Your financial situation might not look so stable in July. You will be bleeding money, and most of the time, this is related to your children or family.

**Love and family.** Your personal life is noticeably livelier, and definitely not calm. In many families, problems involving children are continuing, and there are likely to be expenses related to this.

The stars strongly recommend being attentive with your children, and leaving nothing to chance. This will do much to prevent any suffering on your part.

Most Aries are busy dealing with important issues related to home improvement. You are likely to buy a home or start building one, or at the very least, purchase furniture or items for home décor.

Couples will find their relationship has become very emotional, and not always harmonious, these days. The stars suggest you refrain from making too many demands! Complaining to your loved ones might have negative consequences, and might ruin the best days of summer for you. If something is really bothering you, remember the very useful phrase, "Yes, dear," and hold your tongue. Things will work out better, this way.

**Health.** This month, you are not particularly energetic, and frequently feeling tired or fatigued might lead to changes in your mood. If that is the case, be sure to get enough sleep, and spend more time in nature – summer is the best time of year to be outside!

# August

*It's the dog days of summer, and you're juggling both work and family, and finding new opportunities with both!*

**Work.** You have a tendency to get so invested in projects, that you make circumstances work in your favor. That's what's happening right now – you see a goal, and the planets line up in just the right direction. The heavens are coming to your aid, which means that you are sure to succeed. In all cases, managers and entrepreneurs are able to depend on their subordinates, and employees can count on their colleagues. This is a rare occurrence when everyone works smoothly and efficiently, as part of a team.

Employees will be on the receiving end of attention from management, which may lead to concrete, material reward.

Your relationship with certain friends, or influential members of society, is still less than ideal. The problem still revolves around finances or other obligations.

Things may not look very acute this month, but the underlying problems are still alive and well, and you will be reminded of that in the near future. Closer to the end of the month, however, a loved one or business partner may act as an intermediary. This support might mitigate the situation, but it is unlikely to resolve it entirely- but that's better than nothing.

**Money.** Your finances are looking better, and you honestly deserve it, after all your hard work. You can expect to receive the largest sums on August 1, 9, 10, 17, 19, and 27-29. You will also have some expenses to take care of, but the majority of them are related to something pleasant – vacations, children, loved ones.

**Love and family.** You can expect to deal with some problems rooted in the past, when it comes to your personal life in August. Once again, this is related to children, but this time, the situation is a little less acute, and much easier to handle. Conflicts will start to fade, and right now, that is the best you can hope for.

August is not a particularly joyful month for couples, but they will not suffer, either.

Those who are separated are unlikely to find a path to reconciliation, and things are likely to remain ambiguous.

**Health.** This month, you are full of energy and ready to move mountains. You will likely be able to find a few days and take a vacation somewhere, where you can enjoy bright sunshine and a warm beach.

August is a good time for shopping, creating a new image, or playing sports.

# September

*In September, you will have to prove that you are capable of completing jobs assigned to you. This is the only way to open the door to a better future.*

**Work.** As far as work is concerned, September is fairly positive. Entrepreneurs and managers will be able to promote a major project and earn some decent money. Your team of subordinates is now working efficiently and harmoniously, but small disagreements are highly likely during the first part of the month, though they will not reflect on your workflow.

You will connect with old friends, and influential mentors as well, which will add another ray of light to September's sunny outlook.

The astrologer recommends planning your most important tasks and meetings for the first 20 days of September. The last week of the month, and nearly all of October, you can expect strong influence from Mercury in retrograde. That means that your partners may stall meetings, fail to fulfill obligations on time, or simply not show up.

**Money.** Financially, September will be a good month for you. You will regularly receive money, and significantly more of it. You can expect to receive the largest amounts on September 6, 7, 15, 16, and 24-26.

Your expenses will be reasonable, predictable, and modest.

**Love and family.** Your personal life might temporarily be less of a priority while you are busy dealing with work and money issues. In order to not lose touch with your loved ones and not miss anything important, try to be more attentive and remember that some kind words and a smile can nip a lot of problems in the bud.

This advice is particularly relevant during the second half of September, when you begin to see cracks in your relationships. Remember that things may get much worse in October, and act accordingly. This is very important for spouses and couples.

**Health.** This month, you are feeling energetic and are not at risk of any illness. Many Aries will want to work on improving their appearance and wardrobe or lose weight after some turbulent years. The stars are giving you the green light and promise excellent results.

# October

*Your diplomatic talents will come in handy in October. You will have to adapt to your surroundings and find out who your real friends and enemies are.*

**Work.** After a dynamic, productive September, October might seem like a bit of a letdown. Your negotiations with partners are stalling for various reasons. You may need to discuss financial terms for future cooperation, and that may not always be easy.

Friends or benevolent mentors and superiors may help you with this or other issues, and they will have a clearly positive influence this month.

The stars suggest that you stick to your plans, but you should be flexible enough, and never rush things. Everything will turn out almost as you had planned, just a little later – near the end of October, or November. In some areas, you will have to reach a compromise.

You are connecting well with colleagues from afar, and the results will pay off in dividends in the near future.

Employees will face competition in October, but it is not worth arguing with management, unless there are special circumstances. In case of any problems, your friends or someone higher up in the organization might help you.

**Money.** Your financial situation this month is neutral, but in the near future, the stars promise much more. You can expect the largest sums of money to come in on October 12, 13, 21, 22, and 31.

**Love and family.** Your personal life is very much up and down right now. Someone close to you might go from one extreme to another, and occasionally behave erratically or inappropriately. You will have nothing left to do, once you adapt to their mood. Try to be flexible during this difficult period, and don't get hung up on things. Most likely, it is nothing serious. This is a temporary misunderstanding, and nothing more. This advice is equally relevant for married and unmarried couples.

Young people are likely to fight with their parents, and the problem may be money or other material things.

**Health.** This month, your energy is lagging, and that is most noticeable in late October. During the last days of the month, take care of yourself, and avoid any fall colds and infections. Take care of any chronic illnesses, as well.

# November

*You can expect several serious professional tests in November, as well as personal conflicts. You can't fake your way out of this – there's no turning back, now!*

**Work.** Entrepreneurs and managers of every level will have to defend their position all month. The issue is the financial state of your shared business, and conflicts with associates and adversaries. Most likely, you will have to accept that some of those you were counting on will not fulfill their promises. You will be disappointed by high-level members of society or an old friend.

One bright spot among the gloomy fall colors of this month will be your relationships with colleagues from another city or abroad. You will get off on the right foot, and that trend will continue through December.

Employees should be good listeners and resolve all work-related issues carefully and diplomatically all month, if you want to avoid any trouble. This is most relevant when it comes to your relationship with managers and their assistants.

The best time for any professional event is the last ten days of November, when delicate, challenging issues are likely to be magically resolved.

You will need compromise on all sides, and you will definitely find it. You will get what you wanted, and no one will be left disappointed by the result. Your gains may be more modest than you had planned earlier, but that is certainly better than nothing.

**Money.** Your financial situation is volatile in November. During the first twenty days of the month, many Aries, for various reasons, will lose large amounts of money, likely more than once.

The last ten days of the month are looking very bright, however. Any arguments over money will be over, and you can expect the largest amounts to come in on November 27-29.

**Love and family.** Your personal life is ambiguous. During the first twenty days of November, things will be challenging for couples, whether or not they are married. You might be irritated with each other, or have moral or financial disagreements. In some cases, the disagreements will be related to your children, and this especially applies to couples with children from different partners.

The stars recommend quietly getting through this period, since no one can prove anything to anyone else, anyway. This is not one of those times when truth is born out of an argument.

Trust in the last ten days of the month, when things will be much calmer, and your problems will not look so glaring, after all.

Things will start to work themselves out, so don't pressure your loved ones, and don't make any demands. Soon, everything will fall into place.

**Health.** Those who escaped professional and personal troubles this month might instead face health issues. Be attentive and take care of your body, avoid any fall colds or infections, and take care of any chronic illnesses, as well.

# December

*December is the best time of the year for you, and in all cases, it is the most productive and dynamic month. You are taking the right steps right now, and making reasonable decisions, which will pay off in the near future.*

**Work.** You will have a lot of work this month, and everything related to business and your career will be resolved favorably. Entrepreneurs and managers might complete a major project and implement necessary changes.

Employees will be noticed by management thanks to the obvious progress they are making at work.

Your relationship with colleagues from other cities or abroad is moving along nicely, overall, and you might have negotiations aimed at future cooperation. It seems everything is going extremely well, but remember the old proverb – "every rose has its thorn". That applies now, as well. One such thorn maybe your relationship with a friend or certain, high-level individuals, and the issue will revolve around money or other financial obligations, once again. This will be one of the most difficult issues of December, for you. The problem will be resolved in 2022, peacefully and favorably.

**Money.** When it comes to money, December is not bad at all. You will have money coming in regularly, and lots of it, and the large amounts you spend in late December will not reflect negatively on the overall situation this month. Everything is going great!

**Love and family.** Your personal life is less dynamic than work, right now. You are not facing any problems, here, and your loved ones will not be sidelined. Rather, they will help you in both words and deeds.

Your relatives will also have significant, positive influence in all professional and personal matters this month.

Your relationship with a friend will be a challenge this month, likely near the end of the month, when they will need financial, rather than moral support from you. Alternatively, you might have arguments over material demands.

**Health.** In December, you are feeling energetic, and are not likely to fall ill.

# A guide to Zodiac compatibility

*Often, when we meet a person, we get a feeling that they are good and we take an instant liking to them. Another person, however, gives us immediate feelings of distrust, fear and hostility. Is there an astrological reason why people say that 'the first impression is the most accurate'? How can we detect those who will bring us nothing but trouble and unhappiness?*

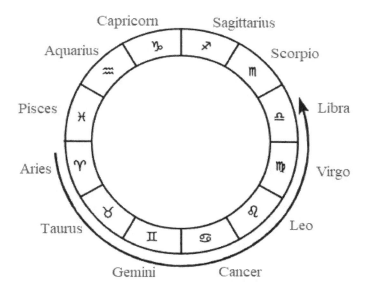

Without going too deeply into astrological subtleties unfamiliar to some readers, it is possible to determine the traits according to which friendship, love or business relationships will develop.

Let's begin with problematic relationships - our most difficult are with our **8th sign**. For example, for Aries the 8th sign is Scorpio, for Taurus it is Sagittarius and so on. Finding your 8th sign is easy; assume your own sign to be first (see above Figure) and then move eight signs counter clockwise around the Zodiac circle. This is also how the other signs (fourth, ninth and so on) that we mention are to be found.

Ancient astrologers variously referred to the 8th sign as the symbol of death, of destruction, of fated love or unfathomable attraction. In astrological terms, this pair is called 'master and slave' or 'boa constrictor and rabbit', with the role of 'master' or 'boa constrictor' being played by our 8th sign.

This relationship is especially difficult for politicians and business people.

We can take the example of a recent political confrontation in the USA. Hilary Clinton is a Scorpio while Donald Trump is a Gemini - her 8th sign. Even though many were certain that Clinton would be elected President, she lost.

To take another example, Hitler was a Taurus and his opponents – Stalin and Churchill - were both of his 8th sign, Sagittarius. The result of their confrontation is well known. Interestingly, the Russian Marshals who dealt crushing military blows to Hitler and so helped end the Third Reich - Konstantin Rokossovsky and Georgy Zhukov - were also Sagittarian, Hitler's 8th sign.

In another historical illustration, Lenin was also a Taurus. Stalin was of Lenin's 8th sign and was ultimately responsible for the downfall and possibly death of his one-time comrade-in-arms.

Business ties with those of our 8th sign are hazardous as they ultimately lead to stress and loss; both financial and moral. So, do not tangle with your 8th sign and never fight with it - your chances of winning are remote!

Such relationships are very interesting in terms of love and romance, however. We are magnetically attracted to our 8th sign and even though it may be very intense physically, it is very difficult for family life;

'Feeling bad when together, feeling worse when apart'.

As an example, let us take the famous lovers - George Sand who was Cancer and Alfred de Musset who was Sagittarius. Cancer is the 8th sign for Sagittarius, and the story of their crazy two-year love affair was the subject of much attention throughout France. Critics and writers were divided into 'Mussulist' and 'Sandist' camps; they debated fiercely about who was to blame for the sad ending to their love story - him or her. It's hard to imagine the energy needed to captivate the public for so long, but that energy was destructive for the couple. Passion raged in their hearts, but neither of them was able to comprehend their situation.

Georges Sand wrote to Musset, "I ɗon't love you anymore, anɗ I will always aɗore you. I ɗon't want you anymore, anɗ I can't ɗo without you. It seems that nothing but a heavenly lightning strike can heal me by ɗestroying me. Gooɗ-bye! Stay or go, but ɗon't say that I am not suffering. This is the only thing that can make me suffer even more, my love, my life, my blooɗ! Go away, but kill me, leaving." Musset replied only in brief, but its power surpassed Sand's tirade, "When you embraceɗ me, I felt something that is still bothering me, making it impossible for me to approach another woman." These two people loved each other passionately and for two years lived together in a powder keg of passion, hatred and treachery.

When someone enters into a romantic liaison with their 8th sign, there will be no peace; indeed, these relationships are very attractive to those who enjoy the edgy, the borderline and, in the Dostoevsky style, the melodramatic. The first to lose interest in the relationship is, as a rule, the 8th sign.

If, by turn of fate, our child is born under our 8th sign, they will be very different from us and, in some ways, not live up to our expectations. It may be best to let them choose their own path.

In business and political relationships, the combination with our **12th sign** is also a complicated one.

We can take two political examples. Angela Merkel is a Cancer while Donald Trump is a Gemini - her 12th sign. This is why their relations are strained and complicated and we can even perhaps assume that the American president will achieve his political goals at her expense. Boris Yeltsin (Aquarius) was the 12th sign to Mikhail Gorbachev (Pisces) and it was Yeltsin who managed to dethrone the champion of Perestroika.

Even ancient astrologers noticed that our relationships with our 12th signs can never develop evenly; it is one of the most curious and problematic combinations. They are our hidden enemies and they seem to be digging a hole for us; they ingratiate themselves with us, discover our innermost secrets. As a result, we become bewildered and make mistakes when we deal with them. Among the Roman emperors murdered by members of their entourage, there was an interesting pattern - all the murderers were the 12th sign of the murdered.

We can also see this pernicious effect in Russian history: the German princess Alexandra (Gemini) married the last Russian Tsar Nicholas II (Taurus) - he was her 12th sign and brought her a tragic death. The wicked genius Grigory Rasputin (Cancer) made friends with Tsarina Alexandra, who was his 12th sign, and was murdered as a result of their odd friendship. The weakness of Nicholas II was exposed, and his authority reduced after the death of the economic and social reformer Pyotr Stolypin, who was his 12th sign. Thus, we see a chain of people whose downfall was brought about by their 12th sign.

So, it makes sense to be cautious of your 12th sign, especially if you have business ties. Usually, these people know much more about us than we want them to and they will often reveal our secrets for personal gain if it suits them. However, the outset of these relationships is, as a rule, quite normal - sometimes the two people will be friends, but sooner or later one will betray the other one or divulge a secret; inadvertently or not.

In terms of romantic relationships, our 12th sign is gentle, they take care of us and are tender towards us. They know our weaknesses well but accept them with understanding. It is they who guide us, although sometimes almost imperceptibly. Sexual attraction is usually strong.

For example, Meghan Markle is a Leo, the 12th sign for Prince Harry, who is a Virgo. Despite Queen Elizabeth II being lukewarm about the match, Harry's love was so strong that they did marry.

If a child is our 12$^{th}$ sign, it later becomes clear that they know all our secrets, even those that they are not supposed to know. It is very difficult to control them as they do everything in their own way.

Relations with our 7$^{th}$ **sign** are also interesting. They are like our opposite; they have something to learn from us while we, in turn, have something to learn from them. This combination, in business and personal relationships, can be very positive and stimulating provided that both partners are quite intelligent and have high moral standards but if not, constant misunderstandings and challenges follow. Marriage or co-operation with the 7$^{th}$ sign can only exist as the union of two fully-fledged individuals and in this case love, significant business achievements and social success are possible.

However, the combination can be not only interesting, but also quite complicated.

An example is Angelina Jolie, a Gemini, and Brad Pitt, a Sagittarius. This is a typical bond with a 7$^{th}$ sign - it's lively and interesting, but rather stressful. Although such a couple may quarrel and even part from time to time, never do they lose interest in each other.

This may be why this combination is more stable in middle-age when there is an understanding of the true nature of marriage and partnership. In global, political terms, this suggests a state of eternal tension - a cold war - for example between Yeltsin (Aquarius) and Bill Clinton (Leo).

Relations with our 9$^{th}$ **sign** are very good; they are our teacher and advisor - one who reveals things we are unaware of and our relationships with them very often involve travel or re-location. The combination can lead to spiritual growth and can be beneficial in terms of business.

Although, for example, Trump and Putin are political opponents, they can come to an understanding and even feel a certain sympathy for each other because Putin is a Libra while Trump is a Gemini, his 9$^{th}$ sign.

This union is also quite harmonious for conjugal and romantic relationships.

We treat our **3rd sign** somewhat condescendingly. They are like our younger siblings; we teach them and expect them to listen attentively. Our younger brothers and sisters are more often than not born under this sign. In terms of personal and sexual relationships, the union is not very inspiring and can end quickly, although this is not always the case. In terms of business, it is fairly average as it often connects partners from different cities or countries.

We treat our **5th sign** as a child and we must take care of them accordingly. The combination is not very good for business, however, since our 5th sign triumphs over us in terms of connections and finances, and thereby gives us very little in return save for love or sympathy. However, they are very good for family and romantic relationships, especially if the 5th sign is female. If a child is born as a 5th sign to their parents, their relationship will be a mutually smooth, loving and understanding one that lasts a lifetime.

Our **10th sign** is a born leader. Depending on the spiritual level of those involved, both pleasant and tense relations are possible; the relationship is often mutually beneficial in the good times but mutually disruptive in the bad times. In family relations, our 10th sign always tries to lead and will do so according to their intelligence and upbringing.

Our **4th sign** protects our home and can act as a sponsor to strengthen our financial or moral positions. Their advice should be heeded in all cases as it can be very effective, albeit very unobtrusive. If a woman takes this role, the relationship can be long and romantic, since all the spouse's wishes are usually met one way or another. Sometimes, such couples achieve great social success; for instance, Hilary Clinton, a Scorpio is the 4th sign to Bill Clinton, a Leo. On the other hand, if the husband is the 4th sign for his wife, he tends to be henpecked. There is often a strong sexual attraction. Our 4th sign can improve our living conditions and care for us in a parental way. If a child is our 4th sign, they are close to us and support us affectionately.

Relations with our **11th sign** are often either friendly or patronizing; we treat them reverently, while they treat us with friendly condescension. Sometimes, these relationships develop in an 'older brother' or 'high-ranking friend' sense; indeed, older brothers and sisters are often our 11th sign. In terms of personal and sexual relationships, our 11th sign is always inclined to enslave us. This tendency is most clearly manifested in such alliances as Capricorn and Pisces or Leo and Libra. A child who is the 11th sign to their parents will achieve greater success than their parents, but this will only make the parents proud.

Our **2nd sign** should bring us financial or other benefits; we receive a lot from them in both our business and our family life. In married couples, the 2nd sign usually looks after the financial situation for the benefit of the family. Sexual attraction is strong.

Our **6th sign** is our 'slave'; we always benefit from working with them and it's very difficult for them to escape our influence. In the event of hostility, especially if they have provoked the conflict, they receive a powerful retaliatory strike. In personal relations, we can almost destroy them by making them dance to our tune. For example, if a husband doesn't allow his wife to work or there are other adverse family circumstances, she gradually becomes lost as an individual despite being surrounded by care. This is the best-case scenario; worse outcomes are possible. Our 6th sign has a strong sexual attraction to us because we are the fatal 8th sign for them; we cool down quickly, however, and often make all kinds of demands. If the relationship with our 6th sign is a long one, there is a danger that routine, boredom and stagnation will ultimately destroy the relationship. A child born under our 6th sign needs particularly careful handling as they can feel fear or embarrassment when communicating with us. Their health often needs increased attention and we should also remember that they are very different from us emotionally.

Finally, we turn to relations with **our own sign**. Scorpio with Scorpio and Cancer with Cancer get along well, but in most other cases, however, our own sign is of little interest to us as it has a similar energy. Sometimes, this relationship can develop as a rivalry, either in business or in love.

There is another interesting detail - we are often attracted to one particular sign. For example, a man's wife and mistress often have the same sign. If there is confrontation between the two, the stronger character displaces the weaker one. As an example, Prince Charles is a Scorpio, while both Princess Diana and Camilla Parker Bowles were born under the sign of Cancer. Camilla was the more assertive and became dominant.

Of course, in order to draw any definitive conclusions, we need an individually prepared horoscope, but the above always, one way or another, manifests itself.

# Love description of Zodiac Signs

We know that human sexual behavior has been studied at length. Entire libraries have been written about it, with the aim of helping us understand ourselves and our partners. But is that even possible? It may not be; no matter how smart we are, when it comes to love and sex, there is always an infinite amount to learn. But we have to strive for perfection, and astrology, with its millennia of research, twelve astrological types, and twelve zodiac signs, may hold the key. Below, you will find a brief and accurate description of each zodiac sign's characteristics in love, for both men and women.

## Men

### ARIES

Aries men are not particularly deep or wise, but they make up for it in sincerity and loyalty. They are active, even aggressive lovers, but a hopeless romantic may be lurking just below the surface. Aries are often monogamous and chivalrous men, for whom there is only one woman (of course, in her absence, they can sleep around with no remorse). If the object of your affection is an Aries, be sure to give him a lot of sex, and remember that for an Aries, when it comes to sex, anything goes. Aries cannot stand women who are negative or disheveled. They need someone energetic, lively, and to feel exciting feelings of romance.

The best partner for an Aries is Cancer, Sagittarius, or Leo. Aquarius can also be a good match, but the relationship will be rather friendly in nature. Partnering with a Scorpio or Taurus will be difficult, but they can be stimulating lovers for an Aries. Virgos are good business contacts, but a poor match as lovers or spouses.

## TAURUS

A typical Taurean man is warm, friendly, gentle, and passionate, even if he doesn't always show it. He is utterly captivated by the beauty of the female body, and can find inspiration in any woman. A Taurus has such excess physical and sexual prowess, that to him, sex is a way to relax and calm down. He is the most passionate and emotional lover of the Zodiac, but he expects his partner to take the initiative, and if she doesn't, he will easily find someone else. Taureans rarely divorce, and are true to the end – if not sexually, at least spiritually. They are secretive, keep their cards close, and may have secret lovers. If a Taurus does not feel a deep emotional connection with someone, he won't be shy to ask her friends for their number. He prefers a voluptuous figure over an athletic or skinny woman.

The best partners for a Taurus are Cancer, Virgo, Pisces, or Scorpio. Sagittarius can show a Taurus real delights in both body and spirit, but they are unlikely to make it down the aisle. They can have an interesting relationship with an Aquarius – these signs are very different, but sometimes can spend their lives together. They might initially feel attracted to an Aries, before rejecting her.

## GEMINI

The typical Gemini man is easygoing and polite. He is calm, collected, and analytical. For a Gemini, passion is closely linked to intellect, to the point that they will try to find an explanation for their actions before carrying them out. But passion cannot be explained, which scares a Gemini, and they begin jumping from one extreme to the other. This is why you will find more bigamists among Geminis than any other sign of the Zodiac. Sometimes, Gemini men even have two families, or divorce and marry several times throughout the course of their lives. This may be because they simply can't let new and interesting experiences pass them by. A Gemini's wife or lover needs to be smart, quick, and always looking ahead. If she isn't, he will find a new object for his affection.

Aquarians, Libras, and Aries make good partners for a Gemini. A Sagittarius can be fascinating for him, but they will not marry before he reaches middle age, as both partners will be fickle while they are younger. A Gemini and Scorpio are likely to be a difficult match, and the Gemini will try to wriggle out of the Scorpio's tight embrace. A Taurus will be an exciting sex partner, but their partnership won't be for long, and the Taurus is often at fault.

## CANCER

Cancers tend to be deep, emotional individuals, who are both sensitive and highly sexual. Their charm is almost mystical, and they know how to use it. Cancers may be the most promiscuous sign of the Zodiac, and open to absolutely anything in bed. Younger Cancers look for women who are more mature, as they are skilled lovers. As they age, they look for someone young enough to be their own daughter, and delight in taking on the role of a teacher. Cancers are devoted to building a family and an inviting home, but once they achieve that goal, they are likely to have a wandering eye. They will not seek moral justification, as they sincerely believe it is simply something everyone does. Their charm works in such a way that women are deeply convinced they are the most important love in a Cancer's life, and that circumstances are the only thing preventing them from being together. Remember that a Cancer man is a master manipulator, and will not be yours unless he is sure you have throngs of admirers. He loves feminine curves, and is turned on by exquisite fragrances. Cancers don't end things with old lovers, and often go back for a visit after a breakup. Another type of Cancer is rarer – a faithful friend, and up for anything in order to provide for his wife and children. He is patriotic and a responsible worker.

Scorpios, Pisces, and other Cancers are a good match. A Taurus can make for a lasting relationship, as both signs place great value on family and are able to get along with one another. A Sagittarius will result in fights and blowouts from the very beginning, followed by conflicts and breakups. The Sagittarius will suffer the most. Marriage to an Aries isn't off the table, but it won't last very long.

## LEO

A typical Leo is handsome, proud, and vain, with a need to be the center of attention at all times. They often pretend to be virtuous, until they are able to actually master it. They crave flattery, and prefer women who comply and cater to them. Leos demand unconditional obedience, and constant approval. When a Leo is in love, he is fairly sexual, and capable of being devoted and faithful. Cheap love affairs are not his thing, and Leos are highly aware of how expensive it is to divorce. They make excellent fathers. A Leo's partner needs to look polished and well-dressed, and he will not tolerate either frumpiness or nerds.

Aries, Sagittarius, and Gemini make for good matches. Leos are often very beguiling to Libras; this is the most infamous astrological "master-slave" pairing. Leos are also inexplicably drawn to Pisces – this is the only sign capable of taming them. A Leo and Virgo will face a host of problems sooner or later, and they might be material in nature. The Virgo will attempt to conquer him, and if she does, a breakup is inevitable.

## VIRGO

Virgo is a highly intellectual sign, who likes to take a step back and spend his time studying the big picture. But love inherently does not lend itself to analysis, and this can leave Virgos feeling perplexed. While Virgo is taking his time, studying the object of his affection, someone else will swoop in and take her away, leaving him bitterly disappointed. Perhaps for that reason, Virgos tend to marry late, but once they are married, they remain true, and hardly ever initiate divorce. In bed, they are modest and reserved, as they see sex as some sort of quirk of nature, designed solely for procreation. Most Virgos have a gifted sense of taste, hearing, and smell. They cannot tolerate pungent odors and can be squeamish; they believe their partners should always take pains to be very clean. Virgos usually hate over-the-top expressions of love, and are immune to sex as a mean s of control. Many Virgos are stingy and more appropriate as husbands than lovers. Male Virgos tend to be monogamous, though if they are unhappy or disappointed with their partner, they may begin to look for comfort elsewhere and often give in to drunkenness.

Taurus, Capricorn, and Scorpio make the best partners for a Virgo. They may feel inexplicable attraction for Aquarians. They will form friendships with Aries, but rarely will this couple make it down the aisle. With Leos, be careful – this sign is best as a lover, not a spouse.

## LIBRA

Libra is a very complex, wishy-washy sign. They are constantly seeking perfection, which often leaves them in discord with the reality around them. Libra men are elegant and refined, and expect no less from their partner. Many Libras treat their partners like a beautiful work of art, and have trouble holding onto the object of their affection. They view love itself as a very abstract concept, and can get tired of the physical aspect of their relationship. They are much more drawn to intrigue and the chase- dreams, candlelit evenings, and other symbols of romance. A high percentage of Libra men are gay, and they view sex with other men as the more elite option. Even when Libras are unhappy in their marriages, they never divorce willingly. Their wives might leave them, however, or they might be taken away by a more decisive partner.

Aquarius and Gemini make the best matches for Libras. Libra can also easily control an independent Sagittarius, and can easily fall under the influence of a powerful and determined Leo, before putting all his strength and effort into breaking free. Relationships with Scorpios are difficult; they may become lovers, but will rarely marry.

## SCORPIO

Though it is common to perceive Scorpios as incredibly sexual, they are, in fact, very unassuming, and never brag about their exploits. They will, however, be faithful and devoted to the right woman. The Scorpio man is taciturn, and you can't expect any tender words from him, but he will defend those he loves to the very end. Despite his outward control, Scorpio is very emotional; he needs and craves love, and is willing to fight for it. Scorpios are incredible lovers, and rather than leaving them tired, sex leaves them feeling energized. They are always sexy, even if they aren't particularly handsome. They are unconcerned with the ceremony of wooing you, and more focused on the act of love itself.

Expressive Cancers and gentle, amenable Pisces make the best partners. A Scorpio might also fall under the spell of a Virgo, who is adept at taking the lead. Sparks might fly between two Scorpios, or with a Taurus, who is perfect for a Scorpio in bed. Relationships with Libras, Sagittarians, and Aries are difficult.

## SAGITTARIUS

Sagittarian men are lucky, curious, and gregarious. Younger Sagittarians are romantic, passionate, and burning with desire to experience every type of love. Sagittarius is a very idealistic sign, and in that search for perfection, they tend to flit from one partner to another, eventually forgetting what they were even looking for in the first place. A negative Sagittarius might have two or three relationships going on at once, assigning each partner a different day of the week. On the other hand, a positive Sagittarius will channel his powerful sexual energy into creativity, and take his career to new heights. Generally speaking, after multiple relationships and divorces, the Sagittarian man will conclude that his ideal marriage is one where his partner is willing to look the other way.

Aries and Leo make the best matches for a Sagittarius. He might fall under the spell of a Cancer, but would not be happy being married to her. Gemini can be very intriguing, but will only make for a happy marriage after middle age, when both partners are older and wiser. Younger Sagittarians often marry Aquarian women, but things quickly fall apart. Scorpios can make for an interesting relationship, but if the Sagittarius fails to comply, divorce is inevitable.

## CAPRICORN

Practical, reserved Capricorn is one of the least sexual signs of the Zodiac. He views sex as an idle way to pass the time, and something he can live without, until he wants to start a family. He tends to marry late, and almost never divorces. Young Capricorns are prone to suppressing their sexual desires, and only discover them later in life, when they have already achieved everything a real man needs – a career and money. We'll be frank – Capricorn is not the best lover, but he can compensate by being caring, attentive, and showering you with valuable gifts. Ever cautious, Capricorn loves to schedule his sexual relationships, and this is something partners will just have to accept. Women should understand that Capricorn needs some help relaxing – perhaps with alcohol. They prefer inconspicuous, unassuming women, and run away from a fashion plate.

The best partners for a Capricorn are Virgo, Taurus, or Scorpio. Cancers might catch his attention, and if they marry, it is likely to be for life. Capricorn is able to easily dominate Pisces, and Pisces-Capricorn is a well-known "slave and master" combination. Relationships with Leos tend to be erratic, and they are unlikely to wed. Aries might make for a cozy family at first, but things will cool off quickly, and often, the marriage only lasts as long as Capricorn is unwilling to make a change in his life.

## AQUARIUS

Aquarian men are mercurial, and often come off as peculiar, unusual, or aloof, and detached. Aquarians are turned on by anything novel or strange, and they are constantly looking for new and interesting people. They are stimulated by having a variety of sexual partners, but they consider this to simply be normal life, rather than sexually immoral. Aquarians are unique – they are more abstract than realistic, and can be cold and incomprehensible, even in close relationships. Once an Aquarius gets married, he will try to remain within the realm of decency, but often fails. An Aquarian's partners need uncommon patience, as nothing they do can restrain him. Occasionally, one might encounter another kind of Aquarius – a responsible, hard worker, and exemplary family man.

The best matches for an Aquarius are female fellow Aquarians, Libras, and Sagittarians. When Aquarius seeks out yet another affair, he is not choosy, and will be happy with anyone.

## PISCES

Pisces is the most eccentric sign of the Zodiac. This is reflected in his romantic tendencies and sex life. Pisces men become very dependent on those with whom they have a close relationship. Paradoxically, they are simultaneously crafty and childlike when it comes to playing games, and they are easily deceived. As a double bodied sign, Pisces rarely marry just once, as they are very sexual, easily fall in love, and are constantly seeking their ideal. Pisces are very warm people, who love to take care of others and are inclined toward "slave-master" relationships, in which they are the submissive partner. But after catering to so many lovers, Pisces will remain elusive. They are impossible to figure out ahead of time – today, they might be declaring their love for you, but tomorrow, they may disappear – possibly forever! To a Pisces, love is a fantasy, illusion, and dream, and they might spend their whole lives in pursuit of it. Pisces who are unhappy in love are vulnerable to alcoholism or drug addiction.

Cancer and Scorpio make the best partners for a Pisces. He is also easily dominated by Capricorn and Libra, but in turn will conquer even a queen-like Leo. Often, they are fascinated by Geminis – if they marry, it will last a long time, but likely not forever. Relationships with Aries and Sagittarians are erratic, though initially, things can seem almost perfect.

# Women

## ARIES

Aries women are leaders. They are decisive, bold, and very protective. An Aries can take initiative and is not afraid to make the first move. Her ideal man is strong, and someone she can admire. But remember, at the slightest whiff of weakness, she will knock him off his pedestal. She does not like dull, whiny men, and thinks that there is always a way out of any situation. If she loves someone, she will be faithful. Aries women are too honest to try leading a double life. They are possessive, jealous, and not only will they not forgive those who are unfaithful, their revenge may be brutal; they know no limits. If you can handle an Aries, don't try to put her in a cage; it is best to give her a long leash. Periodically give her some space – then she will seek you out herself. She is sexual, and believe that anything goes in bed.

Her best partners are a Sagittarius or Leo. A Libra can make a good match after middle age, once both partners have grown wiser and settled down a bit. Gemini and Aquarius are only good partners during the initial phase, when everything is still new, but soon enough, they will lose interest in each other. Scorpios are good matches in bed, but only suitable as lovers.

## TAURUS

Taurean women possess qualities that men often dream about, but rarely find in the flesh – they are soft, charming, practical, and reliable – they are very caring and will support their partner in every way. A Taurus is highly sexual, affectionate, and can show a man how to take pleasure to new heights. She is also strong and intense. If she is in love, she will be faithful. But when love fades away, she might find someone else on the side, though she will still fight to save her marriage, particularly if her husband earns good money. A Taurus will not tolerate a man who is disheveled or disorganized, and anyone dating her needs to always be on his toes. She will expect gifts, and likes being taken to expensive restaurants, concerts, and other events. If you argue, try to make the first peace offering, because a Taurus finds it very hard to do so – she might withdraw and ruminate for a long time. Never air your dirty laundry; solve all your problems one-on-one.

Scorpio, Virgo, Capricorn, and Cancer make the best matches. A relationship with an Aries or Sagittarius would be difficult. There is little attraction between a Taurus and a Leo, and initially Libras can make for a good partner in bed, but things will quickly cool off and fall apart. A Taurus and Aquarius make an interesting match – despite the difference in signs, their relationships are often lasting, and almost lifelong.

# GEMINI

Gemini women are social butterflies, outgoing, and they easily make friends, and then break off the friendship, if people do not hold their interest. A Gemini falls in love hard, is very creative, and often fantasizes about the object of her affection. She is uninterested in sex without any attachment, loves to flirt, and, for the most part, is not particularly affectionate. She dreams of a partner who is her friend, lover, and a romantic, all at once. A Gemini has no use for a man who brings nothing to the table intellectually. That is a tall order, so Geminis often divorce and marry several times. Others simply marry later in life. Once you have begun a life together, do not try to keep her inside – she needs to travel, explore, socialize, attend events and go to the theater. She cannot tolerate possessive men, so avoid giving her the third degree, and remember that despite her flirtatious and social nature, she is, in fact, faithful – as long as you keep her interested and she is in love. Astrologists believe that Geminis do not know what they need until age 29 or 30, so it is best to hold off on marriage until then.

Leo and Libra make the best matches. A relationship with a Cancer is likely, though complex, and depends solely on the Cancer's affection. A Gemini and Sagittarius can have an interesting, dynamic relationship, but these are two restless signs, which might only manage to get together after ages 40-45, once they have had enough thrills out of life and learned to be patient. Relationships with a Capricorn are very difficult, and almost never happen. The honeymoon stage can be wonderful with a Scorpio, but each partner will eventually go their own way, before ending things. A Gemini and Pisces union can also be very interesting – they are drawn to each other, and can have a wonderful relationship, but after a while, the cracks start to show and things will fall apart. An Aquarius is also not a bad match, but they will have little sexual chemistry.

## CANCER

Cancers can be divided into two opposing groups. The first includes a sweet and gentle creature who is willing to dedicate her life to her husband and children. She is endlessly devoted to her husband, especially if he makes a decent living and remains faithful. She views all men as potential husbands, which means it is dangerous to strike up a relationship with her if your intentions are not serious; she can be anxious and clingy, sensitive and prone to crying. It is better to break things to her gently, rather than directly spitting out the cold, hard truth. She wants a man who can be a provider, though she often earns well herself. She puts money away for a rainy day, and knows how to be thrifty, for the sake of others around her, rather than only for herself. She is an excellent cook and capable of building an inviting home for her loved ones. She is enthusiastic in bed, a wonderful wife, and a caring mother.

The second type of Cancer is neurotic, and capable of creating a living hell for those around her. She believes that the world is her enemy, and manages to constantly find new intrigue and machinations.

Another Cancer, Virgo, Taurus, Scorpio, and Pisces make the best matches. A Cancer can often fall in love with a Gemini, but eventually, things will grow complicated, as she will be exhausted by a Gemini's constant mood swings and cheating. A Cancer and Sagittarius will initially have passionate sex, but things will quickly cool off. A relationship with a Capricorn is a real possibility, but only later in life, as while they are young, they are likely to fight and argue constantly. Cancer can also have a relationship with an Aries, but this will not be easy.

## LEO

Leos are usually beautiful or charming, and outwardly sexual. And yet, appearances can be deceiving – they are not actually that interested in sex. Leo women want to be the center of attention and men running after them boosts their self-esteem, but they are more interested in their career, creating something new, and success than sex. They often have high-powered careers and are proud of their own achievements. Their partners need to be strong; if a Leo feels a man is weak, she can carry him herself for a while- before leaving him. It is difficult for her to find a partner for life, as chivalrous knights are a dying breed, and she is not willing to compromise. If you are interested in a Leo, take the initiative, admire her, and remember that even a queen is still a woman. Timid men or tightwads need not apply. Leos like to help others, but they don't need a walking disaster in their life. If they are married and in love, they are usually faithful, and petty gossip isn't their thing. Leo women make excellent mothers, and are ready to give their lives to their children. Their negative traits include vanity and a willingness to lie, in order to make themselves look better.

Sagittarius, Aries, and Libra make the best matches. Leos can also have an interesting relationship with a Virgo, though both partners will weaken each other. Life with a Taurus will lead to endless arguments – both signs are very stubborn, and unwilling to give in. Leos and Pisces are another difficult pair, as she will have to learn to be submissive if she wants to keep him around. A relationship with a Capricorn will work if there is a common denominator, but they will have little sexual chemistry. Life with a Scorpio will be turbulent to say the least, and they will usually break up later in life.

## VIRGO

Virgo women are practical, clever, and often duplicitous. Marrying one isn't for everyone. She is a neat freak to the point of annoying those around her. She is also an excellent cook, and strives to ensure her children receive the very best by teaching them everything, and preparing them for a bright future. She is also thrifty – she won't throw money around, and, in fact, won't even give it to her husband. She has no time for rude, macho strongmen, and is suspicious of spendthrifts. She will not be offended if you take her to a cozy and modest café rather than an elegant restaurant. Virgos are masters of intrigue, and manage to outperform every other sign of the Zodiac in this regard. Virgos love to criticize everyone and everything; to listen to them, the entire world is simply a disaster and wrong, and only she is the exception to this rule. Virgos are not believed to be particularly sexual, but there are different variations when it comes to this. Rarely, one finds an open-minded Virgo willing to try anything, and who does it all on a grand scale – but she is rather the exception to this general rule.

The best matches for a Virgo are Cancer, Taurus, and Capricorn. She also can get along well with a Scorpio, but will find conflict with Sagittarius. A Pisces will strike her interest, but they will rarely make it down the aisle. She is often attracted to an Aquarius, but they would drive each other up the wall were they to actually marry. An Aries forces Virgo to see another side of life, but here, she will have to learn to conform and adapt.


## LIBRA

Female Libras tend to be beautiful, glamorous, or very charming. They are practical, tactical, rational, though they are adept at hiding these qualities behind their romantic and elegant appearance. Libras are drawn to marriage, and are good at imagining the kind of partner they need. They seek out strong, well-off men and are often more interested in someone's social status and bank account than feelings. The object of their affection needs to be dashing, and have a good reputation in society. Libras love expensive things, jewelry, and finery. If they are feeling down, a beautiful gift will instantly cheer them up. They will not tolerate scandal or conflict, and will spend all their energy trying to keep the peace, or at least the appearance thereof. They do not like to air their dirty laundry, and will only divorce in extreme circumstances. They are always convinced they are right and react to any objections as though they have been insulted. Most Libras are not particularly sexual, except those with Venus or the Moon in Scorpio.

Leos, Geminis, and Aquarians make good matches. Libra women are highly attracted to Aries men - this is a real case of opposites attract. They can get along with a Sagittarius, though he will find that Libras are too proper and calm. Capricorn, Pisces, and Cancer are all difficult matches. Things will begin tumultuously with a Taurus, before each partner goes his or her own way.

## SCORPIO

Scorpio women may appear outwardly restrained, but there is much more bubbling below the surface. They are ambitious with high self-esteem, but often wear a mask of unpretentiousness. They are the true power behind the scenes, the one who holds the family together, but never talk about it. Scorpios are strong-willed, resilient, and natural survivors. Often, Scorpios are brutally honest, and expect the same out of those around them. They do not like having to conform, and attempt to get others to adapt to them, as they honestly believe everyone will be better off that way. They are incredibly intuitive, and not easily deceived. They have an excellent memory, and can quickly figure out which of your buttons to push. They are passionate in bed, and their temperament will not diminish with age. When she is sexually frustrated, a Scorpio will throw all of her energy into her career or her loved ones. She is proud, categorical, and "if you don't do it right, don't do it at all" is her motto. Scorpio cannot be fooled, and she will not forgive any cheating. Will she cheat herself? Yes! But it will not break up her family, and she will attempt to keep it a secret. Scorpios are usually attractive to men, even if they are not particularly beautiful. They keep a low profile, though they always figure out their partner, and give them some invisible sign. There is also another, selfish type of Scorpio, who will use others for as long as they need them, before unceremoniously casting them aside.

Taurus is a good match; they will have excellent sexual chemistry and understand each other. Scorpio and Gemini are drawn to each other, but are unlikely to stay together long enough to actually get married. Cancer can be a good partner as well, but Cancers are possessive, while Scorpios do not like others meddling in their affairs, though they can later resolve their arguments in bed. Scorpio and Leo are often found together, but their relationship can also be very complicated. Leos are animated and chipper, while Scorpios, who are much deeper and more stubborn, see Leos as not particularly serious or reliable. One good example of this is Bill (a Leo) and Hillary (a Scorpio) Clinton. Virgo can also make a good partner, but when Scorpio seemingly lacks emotions, he will look for them elsewhere. Relationships with Lira are strange and very rare. Scorpio sees Libra as too insecure, and Libra does not appreciate Scorpio's rigidity. Two Scorpios together make an excellent marriage! Sagittarius and Scorpio are unlikely to get together, as she will think he is shallow and rude. If they do manage to get married, Scorpio's drive and persistence is the only thing that will make the marriage last. Capricorn is also not a bad match, and while Scorpio finds Aquarius attractive, they will rarely get married, as they are simply speaking different languages! Things are alright with a Pisces, as both signs are emotional, and Pisces can let Scorpio take the lead when necessary.

## SAGITTARIUS

Sagittarius women are usually charming, bubbly, energetic, and have the gift of gab. They are kind, sincere, and love people. They are also straightforward, fair, and very ambitious, occasionally to the point of irritating those around them. But telling them something is easier than not telling them, and they often manage to win over their enemies. Sagittarius tends to have excellent intuition, and she loves to both learn and teach others. She is a natural leader, and loves taking charge at work and at home. Many Sagittarian women have itchy feet, and prefer all kinds of travel to sitting at home. They are not particularly good housewives – to be frank, cooking and cleaning is simply not for them. Their loved ones must learn to adapt to them, but Sagittarians themselves hate any pressure. They are not easy for men to handle, as Sagittarians want to be in charge. Sagittarius falls in love easily, is very sexual and temperamental, and may marry multiple times. Despite outward appearances, Sagittarius is a very lonely sign. Even after she is married with children, she may continue living as if she were alone; you might say she marches to the beat of her own drum. Younger

Sagittarians can be reckless, but as they mature, they can be drawn to religion, philosophy, and the occult.

Aries and Leo make the best matches, as Sagittarius is able to bend to Leo's ways, or at least pretend to. Sagittarians often end up with Aquarians, but their marriages do not tend to be for the long haul. They are attracted to Geminis, but are unlikely to marry one until middle age, when both signs have settled down. Sagittarius and Cancer have incredible sexual chemistry, but an actual relationship between them would be tumultuous and difficult. Capricorn can make a good partner- as long as they are able to respect each other's quirks. Sagittarius rarely ends up with a Virgo, and while she may often meet Pisces, things are unlikely to go very far.

# CAPRICORN

Capricorn women are conscientious, reliable, organized, and hard-working. Many believe that life means nothing but work, and live accordingly. They are practical, and not particularly drawn to parties or loud groups of people. But if someone useful will be there, they are sure to make an appearance. Capricorn women are stingy, but not as much as their male counterparts. They are critical of others, but think highly of themselves. Generally, they take a difficult path in life, but thanks to their dedication, perseverance, and willingness to push their own limits, they are able to forge their own path, and by 45 or 50, they can provide themselves with anything they could want. Capricorn women have the peculiarity of looking older than their peers when they are young, and younger than everyone else once they have matured. They are not particularly sexual, and tend to be faithful partners. They rarely divorce, and even will fight until the end, even for a failed marriage. Many Capricorns have a pessimistic outlook of life, and have a tendency to be depressed. They are rarely at the center of any social circle, but are excellent organizers. They have a very rigid view of life and love, and are not interested in a fling, as marriage is the end goal. As a wife, Capricorn is simultaneously difficult and reliable. She is difficult because of her strict nature and difficulty adapting. But she will also take on all the household duties, and her husband can relax, knowing his children are in good hands.

Taurus, Pisces, and Scorpio make good matches. Aries is difficult, once things cool off after the initial honeymoon. When a Capricorn meets another Capricorn, they will be each other's first and last love. Sagittarius isn't a bad match, but they don't always pass the test of time. Aquarius and Capricorn are a difficult match, and rarely found together. Things are too dull with a Virgo, and while Leo can be exciting at first, things will fall apart when he begins showing off. Libra and Aquarius are both difficult partners for Capricorn, and she is rarely found with either of them.

## AQUARIUS

A female Aquarius is very different from her male counterparts. She is calm and keeps a cool head, but she is also affectionate and open. She values loyalty above all else, and is unlikely to recover from any infidelity, though she will only divorce if this becomes a chronic trend, and she has truly been stabbed in the back. She is not interested in her partner's money, but rather, his professional success. She is unobtrusive and trusting, and will refrain from listening in on her partner's phone conversations or hacking into his email. With rare exceptions, Aquarian women make terrible housewives. But they are excellent partners in life – they are faithful, never boring, and will not reject a man, even in the most difficult circumstances. Most Aquarians are highly intuitive, and can easily tell the truth from a lie. They themselves only lie in extreme situations, which call for a "white lie" in order to avoid hurting someone's feelings.

Aquarius gets along well with Aries, Gemini, and Libra. She can also have a good relationship with a Sagittarius. Taurus often makes a successful match, though they are emotionally very different; the same goes for Virgo. Aquarius and Scorpio, Capricorn, or Cancer is a difficult match. Pisces can make a good partner as well, as both signs complement each other. Any relationship with a Leo will be tumultuous, but lasting, as Leo is selfish, and Aquarius will therefore have to be very forgiving.

## PISCES

Pisces women are very adaptable, musically inclined, and erotic. They possess an innate earthly wisdom, and a good business sense. Pisces often reinvent themselves; they can be emotional, soft, and obstinate, as well as sentimental, at times. Their behavioral changes can be explained by frequent ups and downs. Pisces is charming, caring, and her outward malleability is very attractive to men. She is capable of loving selflessly, as long as the man has something to love. Even if he doesn't, she will try and take care of him until the very end. Pisces' greatest fear is poverty. They are intuitive, vulnerable, and always try to avoid conflict. They love to embellish the truth, and sometimes alcohol helps with this. Rarely, one finds extremely unbalanced, neurotic and dishonest Pisces, who are capable of turning their loved ones' lives into a living Hell!

Taurus, Capricorn, Cancer, and Scorpio make the best matches. She will be greatly attracted to a Virgo, but a lasting relationship is only likely if both partners are highly spiritual. Any union with a Libra is likely to be difficult and full of conflict. Pisces finds Gemini attractive, and they may have a very lively relationship – for a while. Occasionally, Pisces ends up with a Sagittarius, but she will have to fade into the background and entirely submit to him. If she ends up with an Aquarius, expect strong emotional outbursts, and a marriage that revolves around the need to raise their children.

Tatiana Borsch